Classic Michigan Flies

Classic Michigan Flies

Jon Osborn

Illustrated by
Joe Van Faasen

HeadWater
Books

STACKPOLE
BOOKS

Copyright © 2013 by Jon Osborn

Published by
STACKPOLE BOOKS
5067 Ritter Road
Mechanicsburg, PA 17055
www.stackpolebooks.com

Printed in China

First edition

10 9 8 7 6 5 4 3 2 1

Library of Congress Cataloging-in-Publication Data
CIP Data is on file with the Library of Congress.

ISBN 978-0-8117-1136-4

For Mae and Wil,
and Graham, Ben, and Maggie

*"People have changed.
We may have missed a lot of it up here,
but I think it's been the most rewarding
life we could have had.
Fly fishermen haven't changed.
Fly fishermen, trout fishermen,
are the cream of fishermen."*

L<small>EGENDARY TIER</small> A<small>NN</small> S<small>CHWEIGERT</small>,
<small>COMMENTING ON A LIFE AMONG ANGLERS
IN THE</small> G<small>RAYLING AREA</small>

Contents

Foreword

About 4,000 years ago, the Egyptians created the first fly for the purpose of attracting and catching fish. Crafted from bone and a piece of yarn, it drifted down the Nile River. History does not give us the outcome of this premiere of fly fishing; however, we know the continuing result. Then and now, humans seem to have an eternal desire to produce artificial flies and other paraphernalia related to fishing.

Relatively little is known about the early days of this age-old piscatorial pursuit, which began in Egypt, moved to Scandinavia, progressed to Scotland and England, and finally found its way to America. For reasons known only to fly fishermen, this method of harvesting supper turned from the necessity for food into an "art-sport" that has grown by geometric proportions. The greatest interest seems to be invested not in the rod and line, but in the terminal object at the end of the leader—the fly.

Fly fishing in America boomed because of the abundance of lakes and streams and the great economic opportunity that was afforded to pursue the sport. Certainly in America alone, there must be a million or more anglers who venture forth annually with boxes of flies to try to turn hope into reality—hooking a worthy trout.

In the early 1900s and even before, many American fly tiers made their marks in history with their attempts to design and produce the "perfect" fly. From Len Halladay in the 1920s to modern-day tiers like Dennis Potter who are teaching a new fraternity of enthusiasts, Michigan does not lack in its bounty of creative genius.

In these pages, we find patterns that have been tried, tested, and proven to be ever closer to that perfect fly.

Wesley V. Cooper, July 2010
Michigan bamboo rod builder
151st member of Trout Unlimited

Prologue

Legends are created when the sharp edges of reality erode and the line between fact and fiction blurs. As time moves on, these icons become larger than life, a process that is fed in part by the human tendency to exaggerate positive traits and overlook flaws.

And so it is with flies. Some of the featured patterns in this book were named after their creators even when their namesakes had little if anything to do with their designs. Nevertheless, imitation is the most sincere form of flattery, perhaps nowhere more so than in the realm of artificial flies. And thus the collective genius of many tiers is often wrapped into one pattern, sometimes deliberately and other times unintentionally. In the end, creative rights to specific fly designs were often lost to the labyrinth of legend.

Perhaps Harold Smedley, author of *Fly Patterns and Their Origins*, said it best:

Flies, that is, the kind we are going to write of here and the kind we use for fishing in our efforts to attract or deceive fish, have always occupied a leading position as a subject for discussion or argument whenever and wherever fisherman have gotten together.

Flies, their patterns and styles, their virtues and vices, their good points and bad points, and the manner of their use or uselessness, have always composed a considerable portion of angling literature, past and present, and they will in the future.

Fishing flies, as we know them today, are the *result of evolution, rather than the invention or creation of any given person* period. Every generation of anglers has made its contribution to the array of patterns now in use. [emphasis added]

Ultimately, the truth regarding the ownership of individual creative rights lies somewhere amid countless opinions. As history deepens, so do the legends of icons like Clarence Roberts and Len Halladay, deeply entrenched within Michigan's grand fly-tying legacy.

Theirs are stories worth telling.

Introduction
Optimists and Dreamers

A dense fog of blue smoke hung in the rafters, and a jovial feeling pervaded the room. Formally dressed men reclined in deep leather chairs while a pine-knot fire crackled cheerily, for it was a cool spring evening in northern Michigan in 1939. Into the night, they deliberated on the merits of particular fly patterns, at times suggesting improvements that the others summarily shot down. Occasionally, though, someone gestured passionately with the business end of a briar pipe and raised an idea that hushed the conversation. Then they quickly cleared away sweaty highball glasses to make room for a vise and boxes of feathers and fur. After dialing up the wick on a kerosene lantern, the expectant anglers gathered wide-eyed around the tier as a new fly was born.

We still have those gatherings. The dress code is more casual these days, and there's not as much smoke in the air, but fishermen forever delight in recanting old stories of how they almost landed an elusive trout . . . *almost*. And we're still searching for that extraordinary fly, the one that will be born tonight and set to task tomorrow, just like the classic patterns of years past. These glorious feathered deceptions will resolve the ponderous questions that leave anglers wanting and perplexed—at least in theory.

Fishermen are optimists and dreamers; the years haven't changed that. But there's still the matter of the fly. It's a timeless fly fisherman's paradox: Anglers search for a fly that better imitates life, deceives smarter trout, and is all the while more pleasing to the human eye—one that excels and endures the test of time. But given the choice, would anglers really want a magical pattern that catches trout without fail? Hardly; all the mystery would be gone. And yet the pursuit for the perfect design continues.

Following are a handful of Michigan-born flies that have endured, even excelled. Most, like the Adams and the Griffith's Gnat, were fashioned many years ago, in the 1920s through the 1960s. Others, like the Rusty's Spinner and the Zoo Cougar, are relatively recent inventions. None of these catch trout all the time, yet they've all proven consistently effective and therefore have joined the ranks of the elite.

Adams

Adams

LEONARD HALLADAY (1872–1952)

It's doubtful that Leonard Halladay realized the significance of this unassuming fly he tied in 1922. A friend and fellow angler, Ohio judge Charles F. Adams, had requested that Len design a pattern for him. When Adams tested it on a pond near Halladay's home in Mayfield, he ruled it a "great success." After fishing the nearby Boardman River, he enthusiastically hailed the creation "a knockout." The rest, as they say, is history.

Toward the end of the nineteenth century, Michigan's fishery was changing. The once prolific grayling had been displaced by brook trout, but their numbers were dwindling as well because of logging, overfishing, and poor conservation practices. Rainbows from California were introduced into the Pere Marquette River in 1882, and European brown trout were planted two years later in an attempt to buoy the declining sport fishery. The browns were especially wary and reluctant to take surface flies, particularly the gaudy attractor patterns used on the less fussy grayling and brook trout. The Adams was among the first Michigan dry flies that effectively lured daytime browns to the surface to feed.

If ever there were a do-all, go-anywhere fly pattern, the Adams is it. Although its namesake, The Honorable Charles F. Adams, thought it looked like an ant, others felt that it mimicked a caddis. In its modern-day dress, most agree it looks like a mayfly, but when tied on a tiny hook, it's a passable midge too. The mixed grizzly and brown hackle implies movement, and the tapered body couldn't look buggier. Although it's not a flashy pattern, there's no doubt that the demure fly has risen to stardom since its modest beginnings. However it's seen, the versatile Adams doesn't replicate any particular insect, but it has elements common to many trout stream flies.

Fly fishermen are notorious gear junkies. Although equipment has evolved over time, the fact that anglers haul around too much tackle has not. Is it really de rigueur to lug six fly boxes streamside when we'll admittedly fish only three different patterns? The answer goes without saying, although it's comforting to have options when facing an unknown hatch. That said, the Adams is a suitable stand-in for any of

Adams

Michigan's mayflies, allowing anglers the freedom to trim down their kit.

Tiers have tweaked and customized the Adams time and again. Current variations include parachute, spent-wing, hair-wing, Compara-dun, Hi-Viz, and egg sac patterns, among others. Whatever its composition, the Adams excels as a searching pattern in any configuration and is the one to tie on when there's no hatch to match. In fact, author Joe Brooks once said, "My favorite admonition to a dry-fly man who has come up against a blank wall in working a succession of patterns is: 'When in doubt, try an Adams.'"

Whether on time-honored eastern brooks, majestic western rivers, or especially on the storied Michigan streams where it has its roots, anglers looking for a fly that can do it all should try the Adams. It's a proud, versatile pattern that has evolved through the years and continues to perform admirably today.

Adams (Original)

Created and tied by Leonard Halladay, 1922

Hook: Dry-fly

Thread: Black or gray

Tail: Two golden pheasant tippets

Body: Gray coarse wool yarn (much bushier than today's dressing)

Wing: Barred Plymouth Rock rooster tips, oversize and three-quarters spent

Hackle: Barred Plymouth Rock and Rhode Island Red rooster hackle, oversize and bushy

Adams (Modern)

Hook: #10-20 dry-fly

Thread: Black or gray 6/0 or 8/0

Tail: Brown and grizzly hackle fibers or moose mane

Body: Muskrat or gray Adams dubbing, sparsely tapered

Wing: Grizzly hackle tips, upright and divided

Hackle: Brown and grizzly

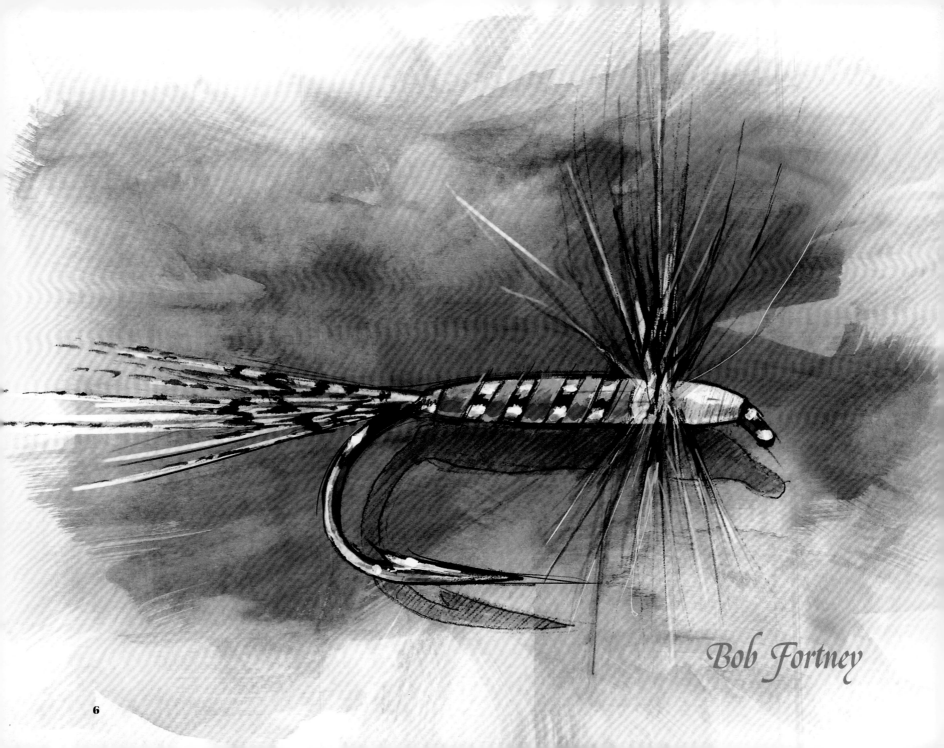

Bob Fortney

2

Bob Fortney

ROBERT G. FORTNEY (1890–1966)

The year was 1932. Franklin D. Roosevelt was elected to office, and America was in the throes of the Great Depression. Jobs were hard to find, and for many, money was a seldom-seen commodity. To add insult to injury, Prohibition would be in effect for another year, making a simple drink between friends illegal and hard to find.

In Paris, Michigan, the district supervisor of fisheries operations had his mind on other things beyond his day's duties. Spring was a busy season for the fish culturist, but Robert G. Fortney was present only in body. His thoughts were consumed by trout and the flies that catch them, for spring is a busy time for anglers as well.

With Opening Day only weeks away, Fortney was eager to complete his new fly pattern, which he hoped would "take trout consistently and last through the years," according to Smedley's *Fly Patterns and Their Origins*. Translation: a fly that not only would catch fish, but also would bestow a measure of immortality on its maker. After he finalized his

Bob Fortney

design, Fortney contacted commercial tier, L. Robey of Newaygo, who produced the pattern in quantity. By 1936, it had achieved popularity on streams throughout Michigan.

Little is known about Fortney's flamboyant fly. Despite its obvious mayfly silhouette, the bright pink silk body and gold rib don't imitate anything in nature. The attractor pattern may have been intended for water that was off-color from snowmelt or heavy rains, as is often the case on Michigan's opening weekend. However, it might simply have been the product of a daydreaming mind when Fortney found himself where all anglers do at times—stuck at work, wishing he were fishing.

Fortney effectively summed up the "why" of fly fishing in the 1930s in *Fly Patterns and Their Origins*: "To me, trout fishing offers the perfect panacea for all troubles, and we have plenty of them today." Almost 80 years later, the world still hosts its share of tribulations, but it's comforting to know that fly fishing continues to provide respite and fulfillment to weary anglers.

Bob Fortney (Original)
Created by Bob Fortney, 1932, and tied by L. Robey

Hook:	Dry-fly
Thread:	Black
Tail:	Variegated wood duck flank fibers
Body:	Pink silk floss
Rib:	Gold tinsel
Wings:	Blue dun hackle point
Hackle:	Plymouth Rock rooster neck feathers (also known as grizzly hackle)

Bob Fortney Wet-Fly Variation

Hook:	Wet-fly
Thread:	Black
Tail:	Variegated wood duck flank fibers
Body:	Pink silk floss
Rib:	Gold tinsel
Wings:	Mallard quill
Hackle:	Plymouth Rock rooster neck feathers (also known as grizzly hackle)

Cabin Coachman

3

Cabin Coachman

JOHN STEPHAN (1890–1953)

In *Fly Patterns and Their Origins,* Harold Smedley introduces his readers to Detroit angler Bill Lerchen. History suggests nothing exceptional about Lerchen aside from the fact that he rubbed shoulders with the likes of Earl Madsen, George Mason, and John Stephan, which is remarkable enough. Madsen was a renowned fly tier, as well as a guide and fisherman. Mason was president of Nash Motors, cofounder of Trout Unlimited, and benefactor of the famous Mason Tract. Stephan, although less of a household name, was a well-known fly tier and fisherman.

Lerchen and this trio of influential anglers often gathered at George Mason's hideaway on the South Branch of the Au Sable River, known as the Cabin. Around 1934, Mason and Stephan endeavored to improve a fly they'd been using for years. On its completion, they named it the Cabin Coachman in honor of its birthplace.

It's clear from Smedley's text that Lerchen was enthusiastic and confident about the fly. "As far as I'm concerned," Lerchen says, "if I were to have only one

Cabin Coachman

fly with which to fish the [Au Sable] main stream, particularly in the latter part of the day or the evening, I would choose a Cabin Coachman. It floats well, is easily followed in the early evening light, and while it resembles no real fly that I know of, it seems to have something which the big brown boys like."

Lerchen also waxes poetic about Michigan's fly fishing: "For a real day's enjoyment, give me Michigan on any of its good rivers, a good guide . . . and I will take a chance on fooling enough fish to call it a good day."

We couldn't agree more.

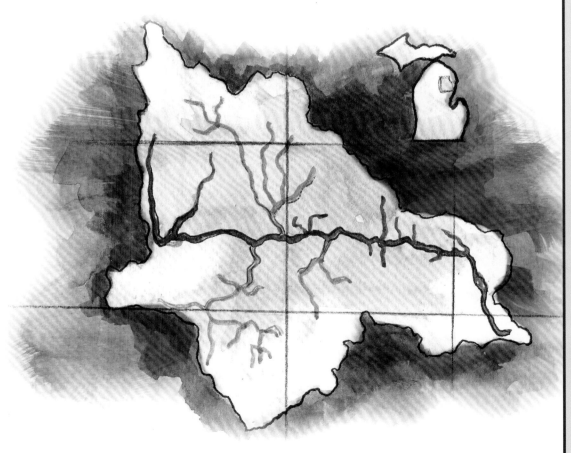

Cabin Coachman (Original)
Created by John Stephan and George Mason, tied by John Stephan, 1934

Hook:	Dry-fly
Thread:	Black
Tail:	Red hackle fibers
Body:	Peacock herl
Wings:	Andalusian, tied spent
Hackle:	Grizzly and brown (also known as Adams hackle)

Lady Cabin
A variation of the Cabin Coachman

Hook:	Dry-fly
Thread:	Black
Tail:	Red hackle fibers
Egg sac:	Yellow yarn
Body:	Peacock herl
Wings:	Andalusian, tied spent
Hackle:	Grizzly and brown (also known as Adams hackle)

Cabin Coachman (Modern)

Hook:	Dry-fly
Thread:	Black 6/0
Tail:	Red hackle fibers
Body:	Peacock herl
Wings:	Blue dun hackle, tied spent
Hackle:	Grizzly and brown, mixed

Houghton Lake Special

Houghton Lake Special

4

BOB JEWEL (DATES UNKNOWN)

The origins of the Houghton Lake Special (HLS) are ambiguous, yet there's little doubt the pattern was born in the late 1930s or early 1940s. Skittered atop the water, the HLS is a suitable stonefly or hopper imitation, but it can also be swung, stripped, or dead-drifted beneath the surface as a nymph or streamer. Presentation aside, many nocturnal browns have been fooled by the fly's tempting allure.

Dave Leonhard of Streamside Orvis in Traverse City remembers fishing the HLS as a young angler: "People think it looks like a streamer, but most of the time we fished the Houghton Lake Special dry. We'd finish the night fishing it downstream to the car. Looking back, it was really the forerunner of modern-day mousing. Not that we came up with mousing, I'm not saying that, but that's essentially what we were doing."

At least three tiers are commonly associated with the Houghton Lake Special—Earl Madsen, Ann Schweigert, and Bob Jewel—which further adds to the fly's mystique. According to Michigan fly historian Tom Deschaine, "Earl Mad-

sen was the least likely [of the three] to have designed the HLS. After Madsen died, his wife came forward and said outright that he had tied a similar streamer called the Buzz Saw, but he was not the inventor of the Houghton Lake Special."

Ann Schweigert, the famous tier from Luzerne, Michigan, is often credited with the HLS as well. She and her husband owned Jack's Rod & Fly Shop, where Schweigert did most of her tying. When failing eyesight forced her to retire from the vise, her apprentice, Dan Rivard, took over. In an interview, Rivard gave full credit to Schweigert for the HLS, saying, "Ann's most famous night fly [the Houghton Lake Special] is still found in nearly all the fly shops in the Grayling area." As Schweigert modestly explained it, however, a man from Houghton Lake entered the shop and described a unique fly but didn't know its

name. He told her he'd lost his only fly and needed Ann to duplicate the pattern from his description. She did so, but made some modifications, and this fly became known as the Houghton Lake Special.

Guide and author Bob Linsenman believes that Bob Jewel should ultimately be credited with the genius behind the HLS, and Tom Deschaine agrees. Deschaine says: "Ann

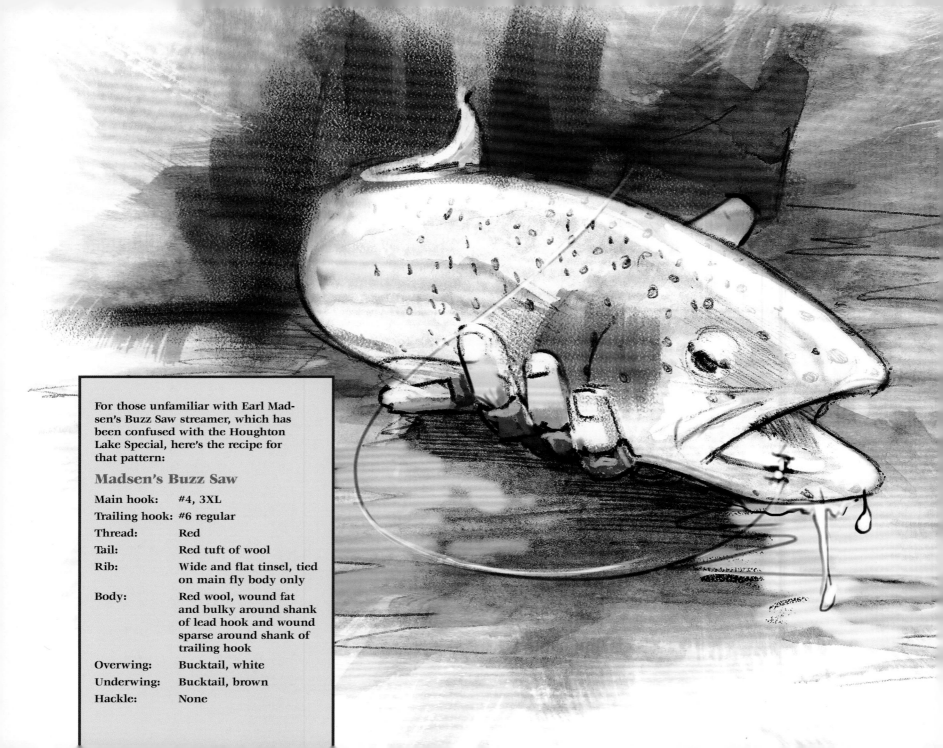

For those unfamiliar with Earl Madsen's Buzz Saw streamer, which has been confused with the Houghton Lake Special, here's the recipe for that pattern:

Madsen's Buzz Saw

Main hook:	#4, 3XL
Trailing hook:	#6 regular
Thread:	Red
Tail:	Red tuft of wool
Rib:	Wide and flat tinsel, tied on main fly body only
Body:	Red wool, wound fat and bulky around shank of lead hook and wound sparse around shank of trailing hook
Overwing:	Bucktail, white
Underwing:	Bucktail, brown
Hackle:	None

Houghton Lake Special

Schweigert admitted that the HLS was created by someone else, although she doesn't specify who." She may have made modifications—she was famous for tweaking flies, but she was very humble and wouldn't have laid claim to a fly she hadn't created. "Furthermore," says Deschaine, "Bob Jewel was a good friend of Rusty Gates' father, Calvin. Cal and Rusty agreed that Bob was the creator of the pattern."

Bob Jewel was an agricultural teacher and later the principal of two Pinconning, Michigan, schools in the late 1950s. According to retired school secretary Mary Ellery, "He was a likable guy and very easy to get along with."

A likable guy, an ardent fly fisherman, *and* an innovative fly tier? Likely, but we may never know for sure. One thing is for certain: the Houghton Lake Special *is* special and thus deserves recognition as one of Michigan's notable fly patterns. It's still found in fly shops around Grayling, where it lures anglers and nighttime brown trout alike.

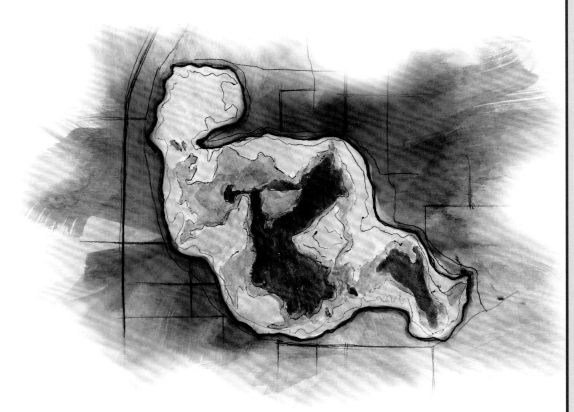

Houghton Lake Special (Original)

Created and tied by Bob Jewel, 1930s or 1940s

Hook:	Streamer
Thread:	Black
Tail:	Red yarn
Rib:	Silver flat tinsel
Body:	Black chenille
Wing:	Brown over white bucktail
Hackle:	Brown, heavily wrapped

Houghton Lake Special (Modern)

Hook:	3XL streamer
Thread:	Black 3/0
Tail:	Red yarn
Rib:	Silver flat tinsel
Body:	Black chenille
Wing:	Brown over white bucktail
Hackle:	Brown, heavily wrapped

Corey's Calf Tail

Corey's Calf Tail

5

RALPH COREY (DATES UNKNOWN)

He was waist-deep and midstream, his daughter strapped in the chest pack where a fishing vest normally hung. Honeybees hummed and grasshoppers clicked on the grassy banks; cedar waxwings swooped and dove in the cobalt summer sky. It was an idyllic August day. His goal was to catch a bashful brook trout—a rarity in southwest Michigan; hers was to splash and soak them both while she giggled.

New to the game of fatherhood, he was proud and a bit apprehensive, and all the while determined to succeed. Barely ten months old, the babe dangled patiently over the water as they waded carefully upstream. Her bare toes, minute and wiggly like tadpoles, occasionally dipped into the cold creek and she gasped in wide-eyed surprise each time it happened.

Today was a baptism of sorts—a sacred immersion into the world of fly fishing. This was very early—he realized that—but if she developed even half his love for the sport, one day she'd be hooked to far more than a trout.

Rings widened on the water ahead, spurring him to action. Some say brookies will strike at anything, but those who fish them earnestly know that isn't true. They can be picky at times, although careful presentation usually trumps exact imitation. He opened the little aluminum box, revealing rows of colorful flies, and selected a shaggy, old favorite: Corey's Calf Tail.

He held his breath, hoping, and gave his best shot . . .

Chances are, Ralph Corey would be pleased to know his creation was still being used. Reports say he'd intended the attractor fly as a brook trout pattern for his home waters near Big Rapids, which he apparently visited a lot. Author Harold "Dike" Smedley references Corey's abundance of fishing time: "Mr. Corey . . . living in trout country, has a chance to practice his particular love with regularity." Like Robert Fortney, Corey later farmed-out his recipe to commercial tier L. L. Robey of Newaygo. Coupled with a light wire hook, Corey's Calf Tail works well on "specks"; lashed on a stout streamer hook, it remains a sound choice for heavy, nocturnal brown trout.

Fly shop owner and angler Glen Blackwood never heard of Corey's Calf Tail until he settled in west Michigan. He learned it was a popular pattern with venerated members of the Indian Club, a private hunting and fishing lodge along the Little Manistee River near Irons. Blackwood had moved from Pennsylvania, an area of technical spring creeks. "Flies back home were tied on diminutive Partridge hooks," he says. Conversely, Corey's Calf Tail is often tied on massive Mustad streamer hooks. Blackwood heard the sentiment echoed time and again within Michigan trout circles: "All you need is a Corey's Calf Tail—that match-the-hatch stuff is nonsense."

Corey's Calf Tail is effective because it is an impressionistic fly constructed simply for visibility, availability, and

Corey's Calf Tail

floatability. Tiers of the 1940s had limited access to materials, and Corey himself said, "I tried for years to get a dry fly that would float. Deer hair would float, but I could not get a variety of colors. When I found a calf tail in white, I began using it with excellent success." In addition to high-noon square-tails, Corey's Calf Tail works well at night when brown trout stalk the shadows and anglers are resigned to dead reckoning rather than sighting as they fish.

Specific information about Ralph Corey and his enduring Calf Tail fly is about as scarce as kiss-and-tell fishermen. Sadly, the origins of Corey's contributions to the fly-fishing community have been lost to time. Of course, that is precisely the point of this book—to preserve similar tales before they disappear altogether.

Corey's Calf Tail (Original)

Created and tied by Ralph Corey, probably in the 1940s

Hook:	#8-16 Mustad #94840
Thread:	Black 6/0
Tail:	Ordinary barnyard calf tail in white and "other colors"
Body:	Red, yellow, or gray dubbing or chenille, palmered in the larger sizes
Rib:	Gold wire or tinsel
Wing:	Single clump of white calf tail, tied upright and leaning forward
Hackle:	Brown

Today's pattern is the same.

Griffith's Gnat

Griffith's Gnat

GEORGE A. GRIFFITH (1901–1998)

6

The pool was tranquil except for the subtle riseforms that disturbed the surface every few minutes. Husky brown trout were feeding regularly, yet neither mayflies nor caddis were hatching. The situation momentarily stymied the attentive angler crouched near the bank. An admitted neophyte, he pondered his options, drawing on his limited knowledge and tactics. The fledgling fisherman knew just enough to carry on a conversation at a Trout Unlimited banquet but hardly enough to do much good on an actual stream, especially one like this, which was slow, clear, and hemmed in by alders.

He finally selected a Griffith's Gnat and, trembling with excitement, cast the offering over the busy trout. Suddenly a hefty brown appeared beneath the Gnat, examined it for a moment, and audibly sucked it in. The angler, in his haste and inexperience, reared back and snapped the light leader, scattering the fish. Who was more surprised was anyone's guess. He later learned that "his" trout had been targeting midges, and the fly he'd chosen—the Michigan-born Griffith's

of Natural Resources) by Gov. G. Mennen Williams. What's more, he was a passionate fly fisherman and an early advocate of catch-and-release, dubbing his cabin near Wakely Bridge "the Barbless Hook."

In the summer of 1950, Griffith met another TU great, George Mason, while fishing on the Au Sable near Burton's Landing. The anglers discussed forming a group dedicated to protecting trout and their habitat. Finally, on July 18, 1959, the two Georges and 14 other men convened at Griffith's cabin and began what we now know as Trout Unlimited, with the basic philosophy that "if we take care of the fish, then the fishing will take care of itself."

Michigan rod builder Bob Summers was a close friend of Griffith's. "George knew the river well," he recalls. "He knew every rock and tree stump—like any good fisherman, I guess. He smiled a lot, but he was very serious about everything he did, including fly fishing."

In 1953, Griffith met with disaster while fishing with Clarence Roberts (of Roberts Yellow Drake fame) on the Au Sable. "George was casting a heavy streamer and hung up on a log," relates Summers. "When he tried to free the fly, it snapped back into his eye, partially blinding him. Later in life, he finally found a surgeon in Traverse City who was able to restore his sight, but by then he was an old man."

Gnat—was an excellent representation of the tiny insects.

The origins of the Griffith's Gnat are surrounded by controversy. The austere pattern was named after Trout Unlimited (TU) founding father George Griffith, but that's where the mystery begins. Did Griffith create the first Gnat? No one seems to know for sure. Some claim that famed rod builder Paul H. Young tied the fly to rescue a tough day on the river and simply named it after Griffith, who was fishing with him at the time, whereas others maintain that Griffith was solely responsible for its design.

Griffith was a textile salesman employed by Wayne Knitting Mills of Fort Wayne, Indiana. In 1950, he was named to the Michigan State Conservation Commission (today the Department

Griffith's Gnat

The Griffith's Gnat is a worthy fly that really shines in sizes 16 to 24, especially on calm water. The palmered hackle imparts a buggy footprint on the surface, but the fly can also be fished sunk with similar positive results. What's more, no one can deny the trout appeal of the iridescent peacock herl body.

One disadvantage of the Griffith's Gnat is that it can be difficult to see. Because of the muted tones and diminutive sizes in which it is tied, an angler needs to have sharp vision to track its progress on the water. For nearsighted anglers, a brightly colored indicator fly fished in tandem will solve the problem.

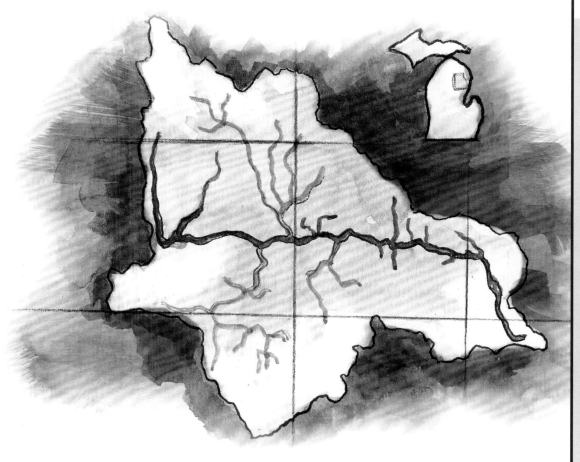

Griffith's Gnat (Original)
Created and tied by George Griffith, 1940s

Hook:	Dry-fly
Thread:	Black
Body:	Peacock herl
Hackle:	Grizzly, palmered

Griffith's Gnat (Modern)

Hook:	#16-26 dry-fly
Thread:	Black 8/0
Body:	Peacock herl
Hackle:	Grizzly, palmered

Madsen's Skunk

7

Madsen's Skunk

EARL MADSEN (1895–1964)

From the split-bamboo rod and click and pawl reel to the gnarled pipe clenched firmly between his teeth, the angler was a personified stereotype and a traditionalist to the core.

His day started like many another midsummer afternoon on the Au Sable's Mason Tract. The July sun was high, and the air and water were warm. As usual, he began by casting dry flies and later swung wets, as was fashionable years ago, but neither method induced many strikes. After scrutinizing his leader yet again, he tied on a diminutive Hare's Ear nymph and fished it on a dead drift, but this offering was snubbed as well.

The fisherman dearly loved to cast delicate dry flies to rising trout, but he enjoyed catching fish even more, and today he wasn't. Rummaging in a tattered vest pocket, he selected a local pattern more out of apathy than faith, for it was neither graceful nor beautiful. Lobbing the subsurface fly against the undercut bank, the angler saw his fortune change immediately, and he was fast into a girthy square-tail.

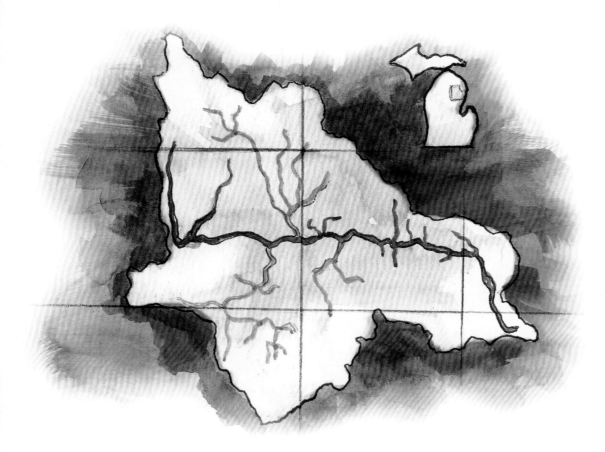

Was it the fly's wiggling rubber legs that prompted this reversal of fate? Perhaps it was the fuzzy silhouette of the chenille body or even the kinky white calf tail—the answer was anyone's guess. Regardless, the fly worked, and it worked well. It was a pattern born near this river in the 1940s called the Madsen's Skunk.

Madsen's Skunk, which also goes by Michigan Skunk or Au Sable Skunk, was developed by Grayling river guide and pioneering fly tier Earl Madsen, a jack of many outdoor trades. He hunted, trapped, and built log cabins, custom boat poles, and cypress riverboats. While guiding, he wore a trademark green uniform consisting of a canvas shirt and pants and a pith helmet, which he used to fend off the wayward casts of amateur anglers. Madsen was also one of Michigan's premier commercial fly tiers and is thought to have been the first to incorporate rubber legs, supposedly made from the interior windings of golf balls, into a fly design.

According to Michigan fly historian Jerry Regan, the modern-day use of calf tail is a recent addition to Madsen's Skunk. "Tiers in the 1940s and 1950s didn't have access to exotic materials, so they used what was available locally," he

Madsen's Skunk

says. "Most fur and feathers came from game that was shot or trapped, which is why you see a prevalence of deer hair, squirrel tail, and pheasant feathers." A riskier and less common source of hackle could be found within the illegal cockfighting circuit. "Those were dangerous folks, but there were some mighty fine feathers in the loser's corner."

Madsen's Skunk is an impressionistic pattern, which is to say that it isn't an exact match for anything, but fish seem to view it as easy prey. Even on bright days, when they're known to sulk among logjams, trout are routinely lured by the Skunk's seductive qualities. While it's no secret that a large dry Skunk works well for after-sunset browns, a small wet Skunk is among the best flies for finicky platter-size bluegills on a warm May afternoon. Another effective variation of the dry Madsen's Skunk is tied with yellow Sparkle Chenille substituted for the traditional black chenille.

Madsen's Skunk Wet (Original)

Created and tied by Earl Madsen, 1940s

Hook:	#2-4 streamer
Thread:	Black
Tail:	Gray squirrel tail
Body:	Black chenille
Legs:	Two sets white rubber legs (8 total)

Madsen's Skunk Dry (Original)

Created and tied by Earl Madsen, 1940s

Hook:	#8 streamer
Thread:	Black
Tail:	Gray squirrel tail
Body:	Black chenille
Wing:	Natural or white deer hair
Legs:	White rubber legs

Madsen's Skunk Wet (Modern)

Hook:	#2-10, 2XL or 3XL streamer
Thread:	6/0 black
Tail:	White calf tail
Body:	Black or yellow chenille
Shellback:	Natural deer hair (optional)
Legs:	White or barred rubber legs

Madsen's Skunk Dry (Modern)

Hook:	#8-12 streamer, 2XL or 3XL
Thread:	6/0 black
Tail:	White calf tail
Body:	Black or yellow chenille
Shellback:	Natural deer hair
Legs:	White or barred rubber legs

Borchers Drake

Borchers Drake

ERNIE BORCHERS (1903–1952)

8

Early June in Michigan is a time when spring and summer waver in tedious balance, unsure which way to fall. Temperatures are notoriously unstable, ranging from frigid to sweltering. What's more, deluges are common, and a sudden cold snap or rain-muddled river sours one's angling prospects. However, when conditions are favorable, June in Michigan offers dense hatches of insects and exceptional fly fishing. All told, it is a fine time to ply the waters. Celebrated author Gordon MacQuarrie was right when he penned, "June is the best time for trout fishermen, as well as trout fishing." Amen.

One of the most anticipated hatches aside from the crazy Hex event is that of *Ephemera simulans*, the Brown Drake. But this burrowing mayfly is admittedly fickle, and persistent anglers often linger into the night only to have their hopes dashed when the spinners retreat to the shelter of the surrounding cedars.

Renowned Michigan rod builder and veteran angler Wes Cooper offers this sage advice: "The trick is finding the Brown Drakes in the first place. Once

the duns pop or the spinners fall, the trout take them with reckless abandon. There's only one exception: if trout have been eating Drakes all evening and suddenly stop, tie on a Sulfur pattern, because the fish may have moved on to dessert. Big Drakes and little Sulfurs go hand in hand."

To properly imitate the Brown Drake hatch in Michigan, prudent anglers should acquaint themselves with the venerable Borchers Drake. As with many other historic flies, its origins are veiled in obscurity. (Reliable sources are divided about the spelling of Ernie's last name. The majority say it was Borchers, with an "s" at the end, but others claim it was Borcher, sans "s.")

Ernie Borchers was a Grayling resident who owned a canoe livery and

prowled the Au Sable River near Stephan Bridge, guiding and fishing with his beloved Dickerson rod.

He was also a first-rate fly tier, and his handiwork reflected classic influence from the Catskill masters. Thus his flies

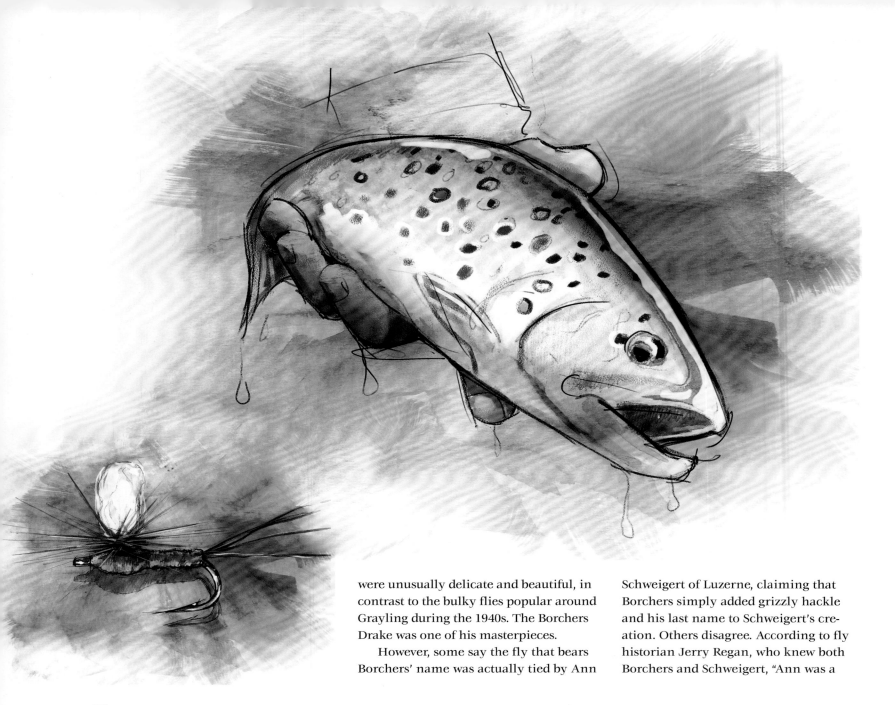

were unusually delicate and beautiful, in contrast to the bulky flies popular around Grayling during the 1940s. The Borchers Drake was one of his masterpieces.

However, some say the fly that bears Borchers' name was actually tied by Ann Schweigert of Luzerne, claiming that Borchers simply added grizzly hackle and his last name to Schweigert's creation. Others disagree. According to fly historian Jerry Regan, who knew both Borchers and Schweigert, "Ann was a

Borchers Drake

whale of a tier and a heck of a nice lady, but she never claimed to have created the Borchers Drake—other people hung that title on her."

Little has changed from the earliest incarnation of the Borchers Drake. The body was originally tied with condor quill fibers, but these have been replaced with turkey quill fibers since it became illegal to possess or sell feathers from condors and other protected species. A variation known as the Borchers Special calls for spent rather than upright wings. Both patterns work well when emulating any of Michigan's dark-bodied mayflies, especially Brown Drakes.

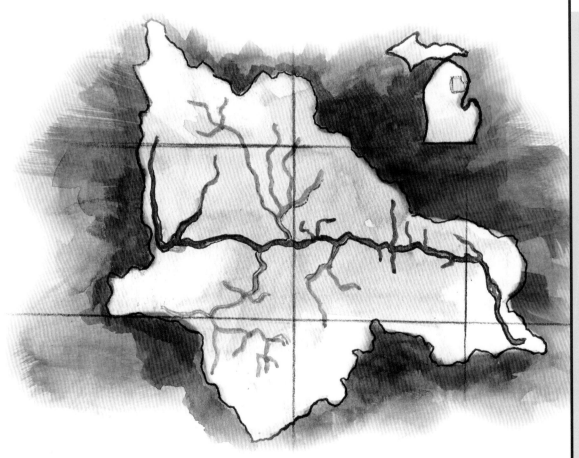

Borchers Drake (Original)
Created and tied by Ernie Borchers, 1940s

Hook:	#10 dry-fly
Thread:	Black
Tail:	Three to five pheasant tail fibers
Body:	Condor quill fibers and, later, mottled brown turkey wing fibers
Wing:	Dyed purple iridescent rooster hackles, upright and divided
Hackle:	Mixed brown and grizzly

Borchers Drake (Modern)

Hook:	#8-16 dry-fly
Thread:	Black 6/0
Tail:	Moose mane fibers, tied long
Body:	Turkey quill fibers
Wing:	Light blue dun hackle, upright and divided
Hackle:	Mixed brown and grizzly

Joe's Hopper

9

Joe's Hopper
ART WINNIE (1880–1966)

Although Winnie's Front Street Barber Shop in Traverse City advertised haircuts, anyone who stepped inside found much more than a fair-priced trim. The enthusiastic banter inside the crowded room nearly drowned out the metallic rasp of the shears. The walls were decorated with rough tree bark to provide a rustic environment, and a carved wooden trout in the front window marked the time remaining until opening day. Men loitered for hours as they conferred about fly fishing, for the venue provided welcome repose for sportsmen.

The shop's owner, Art Winnie, was a respected guide on the Boardman, Manistee, and Au Sable Rivers and cofounded the Traverse City Fly Club in 1913. This talented gentleman bankrolled his fishing obsession by tying flies commercially and reportedly settled his mortgage in similar fashion. The catchy slogan accompanying his inventory of handmade lures and flies pronounced them "A Work of Art." Among his original tackle was the Michigan Hopper, better known today as Joe's Hopper.

Although it was created by Winnie, the pattern was popularized by the renowned fisherman Joe Brooks, who gave the fly a respectful nod in his book *Joe Brooks on Fishing*: "Even in this day of more sophisticated approaches to trout, and better materials for tying, the old, beat-up 'hopper still takes its deadly toll. There are several different ties of this great fly, the Joe's Hopper, first tied by a Michigan barber, being the most popular."

Winnie was reportedly the first to use turkey wings in a fly pattern, but creative as he was, some of his innovations failed. Veteran rod builder Bob Summers remembers one of Winnie's ideas that flopped: "He wrapped clear cellophane from cigarette cartons around some of his fly bodies so they would float longer." This early attempt at lamination failed miserably, however. "It just kept the water in, and it didn't take long before the cellophane hung in shreds from being whipped back and forth during casting."

Although May and June are months of intense mayfly and caddis hatches, the dog days of summer are terrestrial time in Michigan. Hot, windy afternoons deposit crickets, ants, beetles,

Joe's Hopper

and grasshoppers on waters like the Pere Marquette in Lake County, a river famous for its brown trout, which rise confidently to the meaty insects when conditions are right.

Hoppers can be fished in a variety of ways. A floating presentation is the most common approach, with the angler alternately twitching and dead-drifting the fly along the bank. Another method is to fish a sunken Hopper, which emulates a hapless locust adrift beneath the surface. This can be particularly effective on bright days when trout are reluctant to come topside to feed. Still another strategy is to use a tandem-rigged Hopper and dropper, with a buoyant Hopper knotted to the leader and a tiny nymph, such as a Pheasant Tail, dangled below. The Hopper doubles as an indicator and attractor, while the nymph draws many of the strikes.

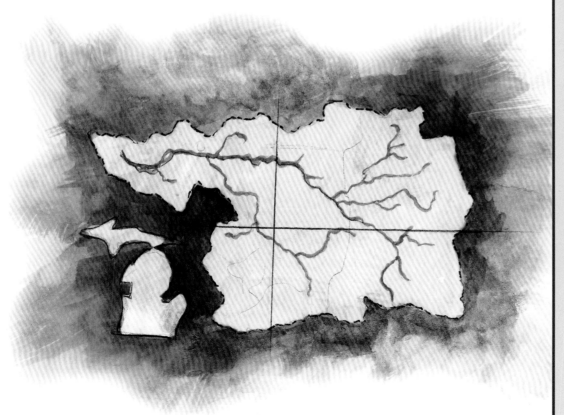

Joe's Hopper (Original)
Created and tied by Art Winnie, 1940s

Hook:	Streamer
Thread:	Black
Tail:	Red hackle fibers
Body:	Yellow yarn
Body hackle:	Brown hackle
Wing:	Mottled turkey wing
Hackle:	Brown hackle

Joe's Hopper (Modern)

Hook:	3XL streamer
Thread:	Black 6/0
Tail:	Red hackle fibers
Body:	Yellow yarn or foam
Body hackle:	Brown hackle
Wing:	Mottled turkey or synthetic
Hackle:	Brown hackle

Roberts Yellow Drake

10

Roberts Yellow Drake

CLARENCE ROBERTS (1916–1984)

With a little imagination, it's easy to conjure the scene. It's sometime in the 1950s, and the venue is a dimly lit Michigan basement. The thick atmosphere is a cocktail of musty dampness, camphor, and a smoky blend of smoldering tobacco. A sump pump drones intermittently in the corner of the room as a group of anglers parley over the finer aspects of trout fishing. By and by, a stocky, square-jawed man sits down under the hot glow of an architect's lamp and lashes some pheasant-tail fibers onto a hook, followed by a pinch of deer hair. Squinting, he critiques the beginnings of the fly. Upon completion, he deems the creation suitable for his home water, the South Branch of the Au Sable River.

The man at the vise was Clarence Roberts, an uncompromising game warden from Grayling. He was reportedly a man's man and a stickler for the rules of the state. The fly was to become well known as the Roberts Yellow Drake, an eloquent imitation of light-colored Michigan mayflies.

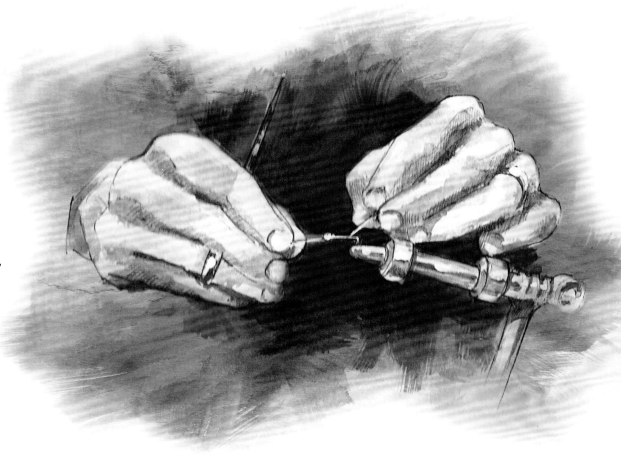

The Roberts Yellow Drake earned its fame for good reason—neither trout nor trout fishermen seem able to refuse it. The white parachute post is easy to see, which is especially important when fishing in low-light conditions during the hatches the fly emulates so well. In fact, according to the late Joe Brooks, Roberts created the fly specifically for his close friend, George Griffith, who was partially blinded in a tragic fishing accident.

By simply varying the hook size and color, anglers can use the Roberts Yellow Drake to mimic Hendricksons, Brown Drakes, Sulfurs, Hexagenia, and other hatches. The parachute design sits low in the film, allowing the fly to imitate emergers and spinners alike. In addition, the Roberts Yellow Drake is tied with naturally buoyant deer hair, enabling it to float without the aid of synthetic materials such as foam, a boon to traditionalists.

Ray Schmidt of Schmidt Outfitters in Wellston is a notable Michigan river guide and fly-fishing enthusiast. He's also Clarence Roberts's nephew. Schmidt was born and raised in Onaway and was schooled in fly tying and fishing in his

Roberts Yellow Drake

uncle's basement. Uncle Clarence and his angling friends, including Earl Madsen and the legendary Fred Bear, took young Ray under their collective wing and cultivated a lifelong passion for fly fishing in him.

Although Roberts had a husky build and large, meaty hands, he tied delicate, precise flies, and quickly, too. Rumor has it that Roberts used his talent at the vise to supplement his state salary, and the fly he created more than half a century ago is still a guide's choice on rivers throughout Michigan.

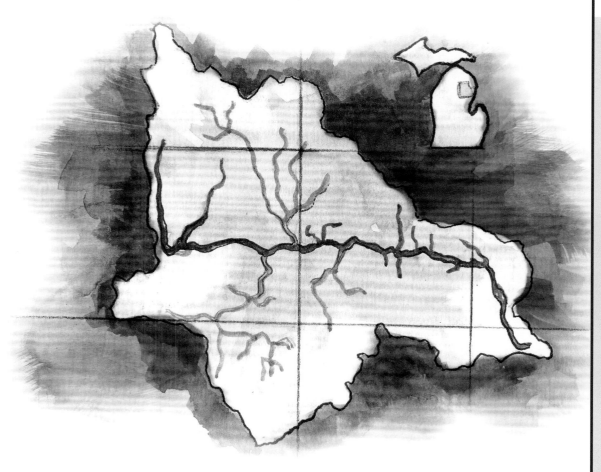

Roberts Yellow Drake (Original)

Created and tied by Clarence Roberts, 1950s

Hook:	Dry-fly
Thread:	Yellow
Tail:	Pheasant tail fibers
Body:	Natural deer hair (records specify hair from a deer killed around October 1 to ensure correct length and color)
Post:	White deer belly hair
Hackle:	Brown

Roberts Yellow Drake (Modern)

Hook:	#6-18 dry-fly
Thread:	Yellow 6/0
Tail:	Pheasant tail or moose mane fibers
Body:	Natural deer hair
Post:	White deer belly hair (commercial tier Mark Lord recommends Orvis Premier belly hair)
Hackle:	Medium ginger

Clark Lynn Nymph

11

Clark Lynn Nymph

CLARK LYNN (APPROXIMATELY 1910–2000)

The sky hung like a lead blanket over Oceana County's White River, and snowflakes cascaded down like blobs of wet tissue. Although it was late March, winter hadn't released its frosty grip on the land. Nevertheless, the presence of steelhead in the rivers whispered the promise of spring to all who would listen.

Tucking the butt of the 7-weight rod under his arm, the angler paused briefly to pick ice from the line guides before re-rigging the setup he'd lost to a fish moments before. Likely it had been a big sucker or perhaps even a spawning walleye, but it might have been a steelhead, dime-bright and fresh from Lake Michigan. The experience left him quaking.

Scratching a kitchen match across his net handle, he kindled a battered pipe to settle his nerves. Then, with hands still shaking, he slipped a strike indicator onto his leader, mashed down a split shot, and knotted on a garish Egg Sucking Leech and a demure Clark Lynn Nymph. With an audible *plunk*, he lobbed the setup into the flow, and the sum of his world consisted only

of the bobbing indicator on the corrugated water.

Although the Clark Lynn Nymph is better known today as a steelhead fly called the Spring's Wiggler, it was originally tied in the 1950s with trout in mind by a field engineer from Oakland County named Clark Lynn. He put the novel pattern to work on Deer Lake, near Clarkston, which was stocked with rainbow trout. The fly eventually found favor with river fishermen and evolved into two popular patterns: the Spring's Wiggler and the P.M. Wiggler.

Seasoned angler John Long of Birmingham, Michigan, remembers Clark Lynn affectionately: "He was a very good-natured fisherman, and he had a memorable habit of wearing a blue aviation jumpsuit around the fishing camp at Edgewater. He enjoyed kibitzing with the guys and being the camp cook as much as he loved fishing."

The simple, yet effective pattern was tied to imitate *Hexagenia limbata*, a burrowing mayfly found year-round in silt-bottomed lakes and streams. Hex nymphs are unique in that they have a two-year life cycle from egg to subimago. During this time, they leave the safety of the muck approximately 30 times to shed their outer husks and thereby become regular prey for watchful trout.

Guide and author Bob Linsenman attributes the Clark Lynn Nymph's effec-

Clark Lynn Nymph

tiveness to several factors: "It's a purely impressionistic fly that works well because it's generally buggy. The hackle denotes legs, and the creamy yellow chenille is an excellent fish attractor."

In fact, Art Neumann, one of the founding members of Trout Unlimited, reportedly proclaimed, "The Clark Lynn Nymph is my secret weapon for opening day."

Be they stillwater trout or springtime steelhead, the Clark Lynn Nymph continues to beguile fish all over the Great Lakes State.

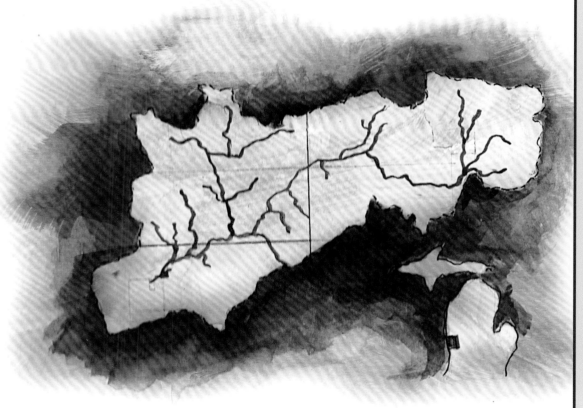

Clark Lynn Nymph (Original)
Created and tied by Clark Lynn, early 1950s

Hook:	#4-10 (John Long's pamphlet on the Clark Lynn Nymph calls for #8 Mustad #79580 or #36890)
Thread:	Light yellow, black, or brown
Tail:	Fox squirrel tail
Body:	Cream chenille
Shellback:	Fox squirrel tail
Hackle:	Badger (preferred) or brown, palmered

Clark Lynn Nymph (Modern)

Hook:	#4-10 wet-fly
Thread:	Various colors 6/0
Tail:	Squirrel tail
Body:	Various colors chenille
Shellback:	Squirrel tail
Hackle:	Various colors, palmered

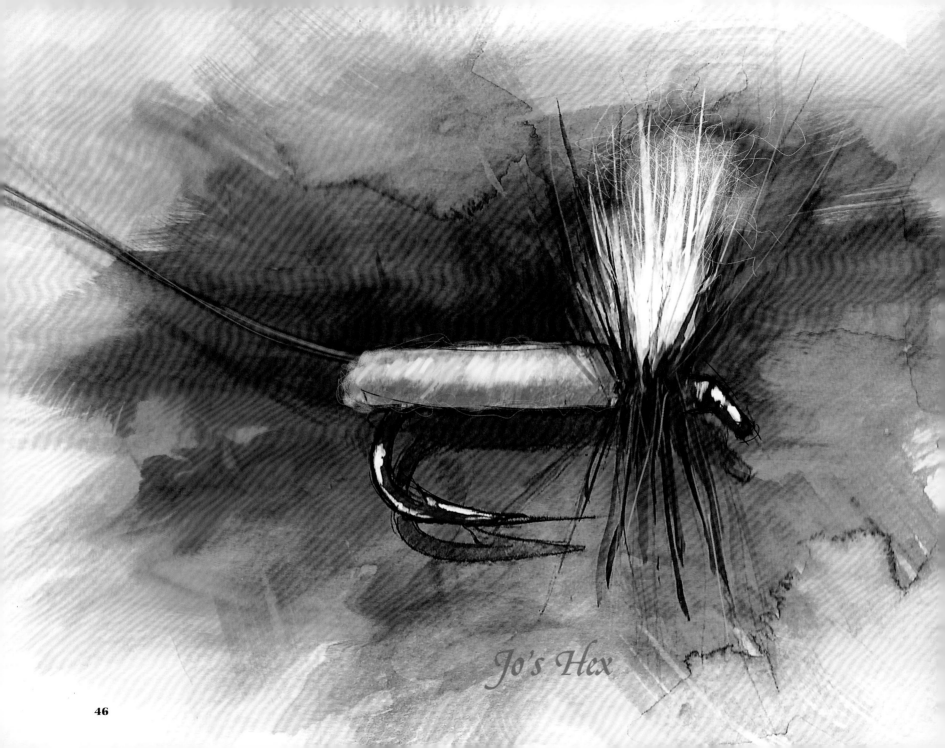

Jo's Hex

12

Jo's Hex

JOSEPHINE SEDLECKY-BORSUM (1918–1995)

With the sun below the cedars, the ravine feels foreboding. Cheerful songbirds have been replaced by the baleful refrain of owls and whippoorwills. A primitive fear of the dark wells up in your chest. Suddenly you realize your nerves are on-edge as unseen creatures rustle about in the gloaming.

Sweat trickles down your face and a cloud of mosquitoes whines in your ears. The homemade repellent—a tincture of citronella and pennyroyal—isn't working. You open the brass lighter with a metallic *clink* and your face glows momentarily as you light the beefy cigar, but the relief it provides will be short-lived.

Then, it happens.

Ushered by the swish of papery wings, legions of mayfly spinners hover and hum above the Pere Marquette River near Walhalla. *Hexagenia limbata*— Michigan's famed "caddis hatch" has arrived en masse.

Gazing skyward, you forget the pesky mosquitoes and turn your attention to the giant mayflies. Before long, the P.M.'s

trout follow suit. Small fish emerge first with splashy, impetuous rises. Soon after, the night is filled with deep slurping sounds, like a fat man sucking Jell-O from a serving spoon. Lunker browns are on the prowl.

You've waited all evening—all year, in fact—for this moment, and you are suitably prepared. Poised with a stout bamboo rod and a smooth-running reel,

her original patterns. None were particularly flashy, but fishermen loved them simply because they worked.

Economy-minded Jo procured much of her hackle from local poultry farmers. Fall found her afield as she garnered additional fur and feathers by hunting resident game. The patterns were then tested and refined on nearby streams where Jo "developed a keen eye for matching the hatches and feeding preferences [of resident trout]."

Summer in Lake County saw youth of all ages working as counter clerks and runners for the shop. At one point or another, Jo figured she had employed most of the kids in the Baldwin area, and staff members young and old reported a happy tenure. By all accounts Jo radiated a sweet disposition and treated the hired help like family—even including them at suppertime with her husband, Ed, and children, Ken and Carol.

Beware to those who crossed her, however. On those rare occasions, her fiery temper rose to the surface! When she wasn't bustling around the store, the small-town entrepreneur could be found socializing at the local bowling alley, which Jo and Ed owned in addition to their famous fly shop.

Jo's varied legacy includes terrestrials like the Top Hopper and a stonefly pattern creatively dubbed the Hot Mus-

you finger the oversize dry fly in anticipation. It's a pattern you purchased from Ed's Sport Shop in the nearby town of Baldwin, a fly they call Jo's Hex.

Jo's Hex was one of several enduring flies created by Josephine Sedlecky-Borsum, or "Jo" as she was affectionately

called. This self-taught "little old country-girl tier" owned Ed's Sport Shop from 1945 until 1992. Although the placard over the front door carries the name of her first husband, it was Jo who kept shop and assumed the station of head tier. Anglers near and far sought after

Jo's Hex

tard. There's even a Light Cahill imitation called the Tan Fury. However, her patterns for Michigan's iconic Hex hatch are possibly her best. Flies such as the Brown Stone, the Lady Jo Caddis, the Manistee Hex, and of course, Jo's Hex, are second to none for fishing Michigan's magic hours in June and July.

Glen Blackwood, owner of Great Lakes Fly Fishing Company in Rockford, says Jo's Hex was a staple of the old-time, big fish, night anglers. When he moved to Michigan from Pennsylvania in 1987, Blackwood remembers Jo's Hex as the premier *Hexagenia* pattern on the west side of the state, and he maintains that modern Hex patterns are simply derivatives of Jo's original.

Years ago, people loved Jo's flies because "they worked"—something that hasn't changed with the passage of time.

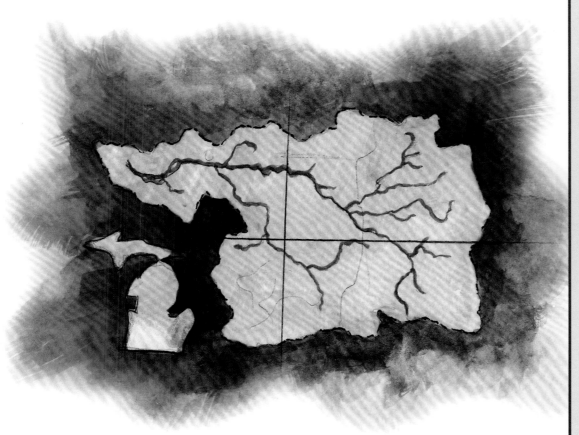

Jo's Hex (Original)
Created and tied by Josephine Sedlecky-Borsum sometime in the 1950s

Hook:	#2-10 Mustad #9672, 2X strong
Thread:	Black 6/0
Tail:	Three pheasant tail fibers
Body:	Yellow yarn with a loop beyond the hook bend to simulate an egg sac
Wing:	White kip tail (calf tail), upright and divided
Hackle:	Brown

Today's pattern is the same.

Beaman's Ghost

13

Beaman's Ghost

HUGH BEAMAN (DATES UNKNOWN)

The angler waited patiently and waded carefully in the waning light. He skillfully manipulated the fly downstream, probing the mysterious shadows of tangled sweepers and undercut banks. Clearly he was adept at this specialized method of fishing and knew that perseverance would eventually reward him. The shrewd gentleman wielding the rod answered to the name Hugh Beaman.

Many fly fishermen harbor an often unrequited dream to live near a first-rate trout stream, but Beaman made that desire a reality. After retiring from a career at Michigan State University, he settled along the South Branch of the Au Sable River, upstream from M-72. In the 1960s, Beaman fabricated a marvelous streamer for brook trout, which he dubbed the Beaman's Ghost. According to author and guide Bob Linsenman, "The Beaman's Ghost is a variant of the popular and effective Black Ghost streamer. The color scheme is what endears it to brook trout—black and gold body, white wing, and red or yellow throat."

Beaman's Ghost

Many fishermen today are quick to debate whether brookies actually prey on smaller trout to supplement their diet of insects. However, the streamer that Hugh Beaman used so effectively on the South Branch sports an undeniable baitfish profile. What's more, anyone who has fly-fished specifically for brook trout can tell you that streamers are among the most effective means of enticing the speckled jewels.

With its bright red or yellow throat paired with a white wing, the Beaman's Ghost is reminiscent of a juvenile brook trout, and the tinsel imparts a modest flash. Although it's rare to find a commercially tied Beaman's Ghost these days, the streamer remains a favorite fly for a devoted handful of Michigan brook trout enthusiasts.

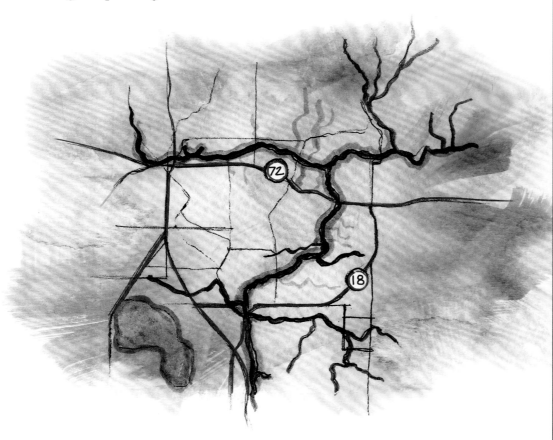

Beaman's Ghost (Original)
Created and tied by Hugh Beaman, 1960s

Hook:	Streamer
Thread:	Black
Weight:	Lead wire
Rib:	Gold flat tinsel
Body:	Black wool
Wing:	White hackle
Throat:	Red or yellow hackle, tied sparse

Beaman's Ghost (Modern)

Hook:	2XL streamer
Thread:	Black 6/0
Weight:	Lead wire or nontoxic substitute
Rib:	Gold flat tinsel
Body:	Black wool
Wing:	White hackle
Throat:	Red or yellow hackle, tied sparse

Rusty's Spinner

14

Rusty's Spinner

CALVIN HUGH "RUSTY" GATES (1955–2009)

The elusive brown trout of the Au Sable River are intensely shy and secretive. These adjectives also describe the late guide, fly tier, and angler Rusty Gates.

Although he succumbed to cancer in 2009, Calvin Hugh "Rusty" Gates is still remembered fondly, and his Orvis-endorsed Gates Au Sable Lodge in Grayling continues to prosper. "Rusty was one of the best commercial fly tiers this country has ever seen," says Josh Greenberg, the lodge's current owner. "Although he was quiet, he was a great conservationist and leader within the fly-fishing community."

Gates created a fly called the Rusty's Spinner in the mid-1980s to emulate the spent mayflies that are prolific through-out Au Sable country. He especially enjoyed fishing the South Branch and felt that the Rusty's Spinner performed at its best there, particularly in June. Gates designed many other flies as well, including Rusty's Secret Rubber Bug; Rusty's Bunny Emerger, or Dust Bunny; and an offshoot of the Rusty's Spinner

called Rusty's White Knot, also known as Rusty's White Topper.

Dave Leonhard of Streamside Orvis in Traverse City calls the Rusty's Spinner "one of the all-time greatest spinner patterns ever invented." Greenberg echoes a similar sentiment. "The Rusty's Spinner is a killer fly from May through July," he says. "It's a uniquely Au Sable design and combines the elements of two very successful patterns—the Adams and the Borchers Drake." Like those famous flies, the Rusty's Spinner lacks clean lines and incorporates several components that trout find irresistible, such as a mélange of grizzly and brown hackle.

In the final stage of their life cycle, certain mayflies lie prostrate on the river in the late evening or nighttime hours, bringing gluttonous trout to the surface for an easy meal. Greenberg points out an advantage of the Rusty's Spinner in such situations: "Fishing in the dark, you have to know that your fly is floating upright, even when you can't see it—but you never have to wonder about the Rusty's Spinner."

Fly recipes tend to evolve over time, but the Rusty's Spinner has undergone very few changes since its inception. "The modern-day Spinner remains true to its roots, except that the initial thread color was yellow and the current recipe calls for rusty brown," Greenberg says.

Rusty's Spinner

Years ago, dying hackle and deer hair was a difficult and messy process. Gates used a secret primrose-colored dye for the Rusty's Spinner. Even though he never fully divulged how he added pigment to his materials, he was always happy to provide swatches of deer hair so other tiers could replicate his patterns.

The Rusty's Spinner took the fly-fishing fraternity by storm a quarter century ago, and it's still wildly popular with guides and anglers. Rusty Gates' amazing legacy lives on through his lodge, conservation efforts, and innovative flies.

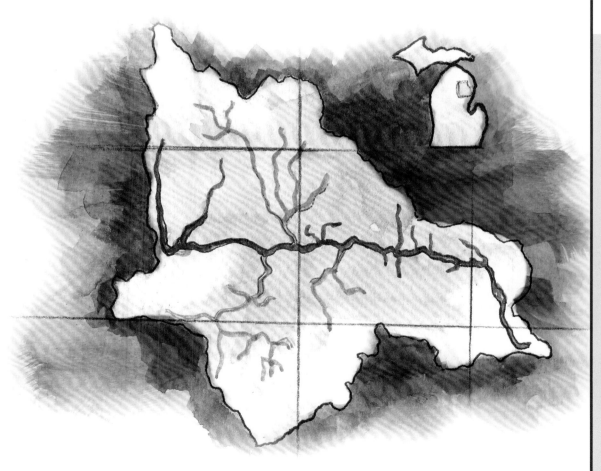

Rusty's Spinner (Original)
Created and tied by Rusty Gates, mid-1980s

Hook:	Dry-fly
Thread:	Yellow
Tail:	Moose mane
Body:	Dyed rusty brown deer hair, tied parallel to the hook shank
Wings:	Grizzly hen, three-quarters spent
Hackle:	Grizzly and brown

Rusty's Spinner (Modern)

Hook:	#6-18 dry-fly
Thread:	Rusty brown
Tail:	Moose mane
Body:	Dyed rusty brown deer hair, tied parallel to the hook shank
Wings:	Grizzly hen, three-quarters spent
Hackle:	Grizzly and brown

Circus Peanut

15

Circus Peanut

RUSS MADDIN (1976–)

Midmorning in the Troutsman Fly Shop had guides Russ Maddin and Kelly Galloup pondering a problem over a fourth cup of black coffee. Lately they'd been experimenting with new streamer patterns tied on long-shank Carrie Stevens-style hooks. The fish had shown interest, but something still wasn't right; clients weren't getting solid hookups. Somewhere between the bite and the boat, the trout were coming unpinned.

Maddin remembers the era well. "We were hooking donkeys (huge trout) left and right but losing a lot of them—they were just spinning off the hook. One decent gator roll and they'd be gone."

Back at the vise, Maddin held the traditional streamer hook between his thumb and forefinger and scrutinized it for the umpteenth time. Suddenly it dawned on him: When the trout rolled, as browns often do, the long hook provided too much leverage, which allowed them to pop free. As a solution, Maddin envisioned an articulated fly constructed of a pair of short hooks instead of the single, long hook he'd been using.

The end-result would be known as the venerable Circus Peanut, a fly which rivals Galloup's famous Zoo Cougar as one of the most influential and effective streamers of all time. But make no mistake: the pattern was not simply the product of a single, caffeine-charged brainstorming session. Instead it was the culmination of angling experience and years at the vise.

Step back, if you will, to 1984. Eight-year old Russ Maddin had been left in the care of family friends while his folks were in Africa on business. The caring couple bought young Maddin a beginner's fly-tying kit, and he dove in with the fervor of a religious convert. When he'd depleted all the dubbing and chenille that came with the kit, Maddin pilfered cotton balls and dental floss from the family medicine cabinet. He just couldn't get enough.

Surprisingly at that time, Maddin hadn't ever fished—even with lures or bait. When the preteen finally took up fly fishing, the "line" he used was actually Dacron backing—he didn't know any different. "I was like Hacksaw Jim

Duggan," he says ruefully, comparing his casting to the 2x4-swinging 1980s wrestler. Handicapped by his gear, he struggled to learn proper technique until a friend bailed him out with an old coil of Cortland 444 line. "It was like going from a Pinto to a Maserati," Maddin admits.

Thus began a life rooted in fly fishing. From the suburbs of Detroit to rural upper Michigan, Maddin's passion has taken him from the Riverbend Fly Shop

on the detritus of each river system. "If the fly literally disappears when it hits the water, it's going to fish well," Maddin says confidently.

The placement of the dumbbell eyes is also important. Lashed on top of the hook shank, the eyes will impart a jig-like action, similar to that of a Clouser Minnow. Problem is, Clousers don't cast well. If acceleration and distance are the goal, the eyes must be tied underneath the hook to make the fly easier to cast and more accurate.

Probably most important of all is the Circus Peanut's articulated design. Using two short-shank hooks joined together by heavy monofilament imparts movement and solves the leverage issue that proved so problematic with the traditional Carrie Stevens hooks.

While each carefully considered element is part and parcel to the Circus Peanut's universal appeal, the wiggling rubber legs, sparkling Krystal Flash, and undulating schlappen and marabou also contribute to its effectiveness.

Maddin's catalog of flies includes the South Bound Trucker, the Mad Pup, and the Krakin, among others. But where did the name Circus Peanut come from? Maddin explains with a chuckle: "After I tied the first Peanut, a buddy shook his head while looking it over and scoffed, 'That thing is so nappy it looks like a circus act—like a freak show!'"

as a teenager to Hawkins Outfitters, where he currently guides, and a handful of others in between.

Despite the passage of years, Maddin's passion for guiding and creating cutting-edge flies burns hotter than ever. He's been known to study the action of balsa baitfish lures like Rapalas to enhance his streamer designs. "Little things like keels or counterweight on the bend of the hook can make all the difference on a fly," he claims.

Maddin says the Circus Peanut's success is based on several factors: "Matching the fly to the river bottom is key," he instructs. He bases his patterns' colors

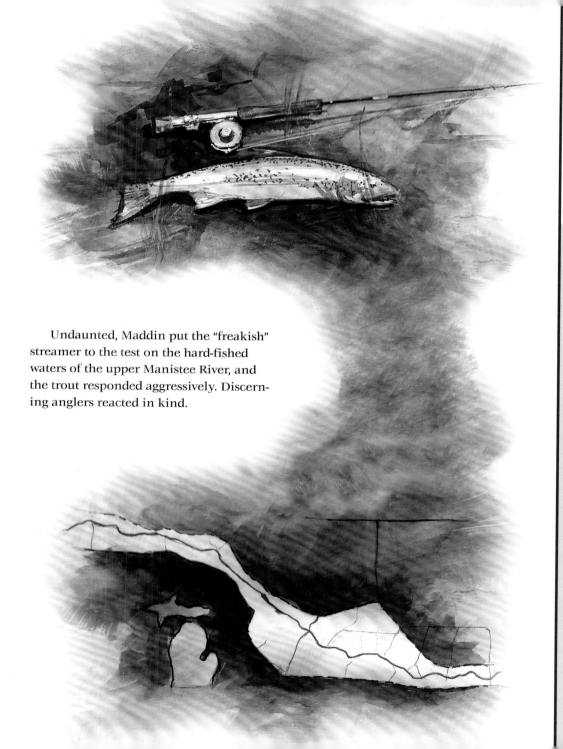

Undaunted, Maddin put the "freakish" streamer to the test on the hard-fished waters of the upper Manistee River, and the trout responded aggressively. Discerning anglers reacted in kind.

Circus Peanut (Original)

Created and tied by Russ Maddin in 2002

Thread:	Black 6/0
Hooks:	#2-4 TMC #5262 or #5263 (rear hook) and TMC #9395 (front hook, size matched to rear hook)
Tail:	Sculpin-olive marabou and copper Flashabou
Legs:	Barred chartreuse or barred pumpkinseed Sili Legs
Body:	Rootbeer Estaz
Head:	Rootbeer Estaz, three figure eight wraps with optional schlappen hackle, rubber legs, and more hackle if desired
Hackle:	Brown schlappen (1½ turns using fluff at bottom of feather)
Connection:	30-pound Maxima doubled-over

Today's pattern is the same.

Zoo Cougar

KELLY GALLOUP (1959–)

April rains and snowmelt had bloated the legendary Manistee River, or "Big Man," as it's locally known. A bulky deer hair streamer fluttered and jerked through the turbid waters, which were stained the color of the weak coffee served on Sundays in church basements throughout the Wolverine State. Although the fly, a locally tied Zoo Cougar, was visually obscured, its wide head displaced water as it surged in the current, and the vibrations drew the attention of a brag-worthy brown trout. The winter-hungry predator flashed from its lair and seized the faux sculpin. No sooner had the fish taken the fly into its gaping maw than the angler set the hook and the battle was on.

While many fly fishermen are drawn to the pastoral allure of dry flies, it's no secret that catching trophy-size trout often requires the use of streamers. The fact is, when trout reach a certain size—many experts say 14 inches—their diet switches from insects to smaller fish and crustaceans. Streamers imitate baitfish, leeches, and crayfish and stimulate large

fish to bite because of predatory or territorial instincts.

Kelly Galloup, living legend and originator of the famed Zoo Cougar, designed the streamer in 1996 for the Manistee River. He wanted a sculpin pattern that could be fished just under the surface. Galloup originally dubbed the fly the Manistee Muddler, tying it unweighted and intending it to be paired with a sinking line, thereby allowing it to undulate at the mercy of the currents like an injured baitfish. Galloup maintains that these factors allow for the realistic action that has proven enticing to large, cannibalistic brown trout. Although the initial color was yellow, the Cougar is now also tied in black, olive, tan, gray, and golden brown. Galloup says he hasn't made any other deviations from the original pattern.

A native of Michigan, Galloup was once the proprietor of the Troutsman fly shop in Traverse City. He currently owns Galloup's Slide Inn on the Madison River in Cameron, Montana. Although he no longer calls Michigan home, Gal-

Zoo Cougar

loup continues to fish the Zoo Cougar with great results west of the Rockies.

"Montana water is grand, but there is an intimacy to rivers with shadows like the Manistee in Michigan," he wistfully admits. "The Zoo Cougar is still my go-to fly and more often the one I'm using when I find myself 'wreckin' house.'" He also relates that one of his best days on *any* river was when he first tested the Zoo Cougar with Michigan guide Bob Linsenman. On that unprecedented float, the two anglers collectively landed 13 browns over 20 inches. The trout weren't the only ones hooked. Galloup says the fly is among the best he's ever produced.

Zoo Cougar (Original)

Created and tied by Kelly Galloup, 1996

Hook:	#4-10 TMC 300
Thread:	Yellow GSP 100 or monocord
Tail:	Dyed yellow marabou
Body:	Pearl Sparkle Braid
Underwing:	White calf tail
Wing:	Dyed yellow mallard flank
Collar:	Dyed yellow deer hair
Head:	Dyed yellow deer hair, cut and shaped

Zoo Cougar (Modern)

Hook:	#4-10 TMC 300
Thread:	Yellow, black, olive, tan, gray, or golden brown GSP 100 or monocord
Tail:	Dyed yellow, black, olive, tan, gray, or golden brown marabou
Body:	Pearl Sparkle Braid
Underwing:	White calf tail
Wing:	Mallard flank
Collar:	Dyed yellow, black, olive, tan, gray, or golden brown deer hair
Head:	Dyed yellow, black, olive, tan, gray, or brown deer hair, cut and shaped

Conclusion

Nearly a century has passed since Len Halladay first tied his iconic fly. With the help of families, friends, and associates of the original tiers, we set out to preserve the chronicles of the Adams and other classic patterns, lest they be lost to the hands of time. It would be easy to assume that the fly-fishing community would always remember their stories, but fly fishermen can be prone to memory loss. Just ask any serious angler the whereabouts of a trophy trout!

With the passage of years comes change, and Michigan's fly-fishing community is hardly exempt. For example, Grayling is the name of a trout town, but the label once described an eager, iridescent fish, largely extinct from its native waters for nearly a century. Moreover, today's brown trout are basically natives, no longer Loch Leven immigrants from Germany as they were in the late 1800s. Brook trout these days are noticeably smaller on average than those caught once-upon-a-time by anglers like Clarence Roberts. Depending on the creek, a foot-long

fish qualifies as a trophy, and one over 20 inches is almost unheard of. Crowded conditions, pollution, overfishing, habitat loss, warming streams . . . these are only some of the issues facing modern-day fly fishermen.

Yet thanks to organizations like Trout Unlimited, Michigan still boasts world-class rivers such as the Au Sable, Pere Marquette, and Manistee, to name just a few. Furthermore, countless tributaries, their names spoken only in hushed tones, noodle across the state and are quietly famous in their own right. Bashful brookies hide in covert trickles, and trophy browns lie in storied after-dark pools. Each year, anadromous monsters from the Great Lakes traverse undammed sections of rivers and creeks to ensure that their species continues. Enthusiasts still gather in local shops, basements, and dens all over the state to tie flies—some new innovations, but the classics too. It's safe to assume that these facts alone would have pleased the likes of George Griffith and Earl Madsen.

On the heels of modern pioneers like Rusty Gates and Kelly Galloup, a

new generation of tiers is creating revolutionary flies even as you read this. Fresh techniques and the availability of quality materials have revolutionized fly production. Synthetic components, such as rubber legs and foam, and innovations like articulated and extended bodies have allowed for patterns that would have been unthinkable during the heyday of the Old Masters. Whereas sizes 10 or 12 were the impressionistic norm in the early 1900s, modern-day flies are comparably diminutive, with realistic imitations from 16 to 18 being average, with some infinitely smaller. In turn, fly tying and therefore fly fishing are headed in a whole new direction, yet the art aspect of both disciplines remains firmly intact.

Admittedly, times have changed since Art Winnie and Ernie Borchers engineered the cutting-edge flies of their eras. Nevertheless, a close look at the patterns and tiers of today reveals a continuation of the grand fly-tying legacy that began decades ago and likely will continue for many years to come.

Acknowledgments

Thanks to Joe for his focused creativity and the late-night, bourbon-fueled discussions that saw this project to completion. Thanks to my wife, Angela, and my kids, Mae and Wil, for their patience through the lengthy interviews, and for understanding my escapes to the river.

Thanks to Jay Nichols and Stackpole Books for guiding us through this project. And to Tom Carney of the *Upland Almanac* for providing a platform for my writing and author Jerry Dennis for his advice on this specific project.

Finally, I'd like to thank my mom for instilling in me the love of reading and my dad for passing on his enthusiasm for fishing and the outdoors. These are gifts that money cannot buy.

—Jon Osborn

Thanks to Jon for his tireless research and his commitment to make these stories come to life. To my parents for the years of consistent encouragement as I pursued a career in art and design. And lastly a big thanks to my wife Emily for enduring all the fly-fishing chatter, for her honest critiques, and most of all, for her unwavering support.

—Joe Van Faasen

The author also wishes to thank the following people who gave generously of their time and shared their expertise.

Glen Blackwood of Great Lakes Fly Fishing Company in Rockford provided information about Jo's Hex and Corey's Calf Tail.

Julie Borak is a volunteer at the Au Sable River Center in Roscommon. She provided a *Michigan-Out-of-Doors* article about the Houghton Lake Special.

Jamie Clous of Old Au Sable Fly Shop is one of Michigan's top guides. He led us to some of the Au Sable's historic stretches, which still produce trout of epic proportions, and gave technical assistance on modern flies.

Wesley V. Cooper owns Cooper's Fly Rods in Fremont and graciously wrote the forward and provided hatch knowledge for the Roberts Yellow Drake.

Jerry Dennis is an author and angler in Traverse City and a driving force behind the completion of this project.

Tom Deschaine is a fly historian and author in Westland who shared historical and technical knowledge on the Adams, Griffith's Gnat, Roberts Yellow Drake, Joe's Hopper, Houghton Lake Special, Jo's Hex, and Corey's Calf Tail.

Mary Ellery is a retired secretary of the Pinconning Schools Superintendent's Office and provided information on Bob Jewel.

Kelly Galloup is a guide and author, as well as the owner of Galloup's Slide Inn in Cameron, Montana. He shared historical and technical knowledge on his Zoo Cougar pattern.

Josh Greenberg is the owner of Gates Au Sable Lodge in Grayling. He provided historical and technical knowledge on Rusty's Spinner.

Dave Leonhard of Streamside Orvis in Traverse City shared information on the Houghton Lake Special, Rusty's Spinner, Roberts Yellow Drake, Borchers Drake, Clark Lynn Nymph, and Madsen's Skunk.

Bob Linsenman is an author and angler, as well as the owner of Bob Linsenman's Au Sable Angler. He shared historical knowledge on the Houghton Lake Special, Beaman's Ghost, and Clark Lynn Nymph.

John J. P. Long is an angler and friend of the late Clark Lynn who lives in Birmingham. He authored a pamphlet on the Clark Lynn Nymph and provided additional information on the fly.

Mark Lord is a commercial fly tier in Kingsley who shared clippings from the *Michigan-Out-of-Doors* articles as well as detailed information on the Adams, Roberts Yellow Drake, Borchers Drake, Madson's Skunk, Joe's Hopper, Rusty's Spinner, and Houghton Lake Special.

Russ Maddin, production fly tier and guide at Hawkins Outfitters in Lake Ann, provided information on the Circus Peanut.

Lovells Museum shared information on Ernie Borchers, Clarence Roberts, Earl Madsen, George Griffith, Clark Lynn, Rusty Gates, and many other icons of Michigan fly-fishing history.

Andy Partlo of Old Au Sable Fly Shop in Grayling shared his technical knowledge and provided referrals to people like Jerry Regan and Jamie Clous.

Jerry Regan is a fly historian and commercial tier in Grayling. He provided historical and technical knowledge on the Adams, Roberts Yellow Drake, Griffith's Gnat, Madsen's Skunk, and Borchers Drake.

Ray Schmidt of Schmidt Outfitters in Wellston is a guide, angler, and author who provided information about his uncle, Clarence Roberts, and the Roberts Yellow Drake.

Bob Summers of R. W. Summers Company in Traverse City, maker of fine Tonkin cane rods, shared his historical and technical knowledge on the Griffith's Gnat, Roberts Yellow Drake, and Joe's Hopper.

Bob Ward of Clarkston, Michigan, provided information on the Clark Lynn Nymph.

References

Brooks, Joe. *The Complete Book of Fly Fishing*. New York: Outdoor Life, 1958.

———. *Trout Fishing*. New York: Harper & Row, 1972.

Deschaine, Tom. "Jo's Flies." *Michigan Dry Flies*. 2011. http://www.michigandry flies.net.

———. "Josephine Sedlecky-Borsum—First Lady of the Vice." *Fly Anglers Online*. 2011. http://www.flyanglersonline.com.

Hendrickson, Gerth E. *Twelve Classic Trout Streams in Michigan*. 3rd ed. Ann Arbor: University of Michigan Press, 2009.

Linsenman, Bob. "Ten Great Michigan Flies." *Michigan's Streamside Journal*. http://www .michigansstreamsidejournal.com/issues/issue5.html.

Long, John J. P. *The Clark Lynn Nymph*, a pamphlet published independently from, but included in his 1987 compilation, *Emergence Schedule—A Complete Guide to Matching the Insect Hatches of Michigan Trout Streams*, written for the Challenge Chapter of Trout Unlimited.

MacQuarrie, Gordon. *The Gordon MacQuarrie Sporting Treasury*. Compiled and edited by Zack Taylor. Minocqua, WI: Willow Creek Press, 1998.

Pomeroy, Dick. "Michigan Fly Box." *Michigan Out-of-Doors Magazine*. August 1984, August 1990, & September 1994.

Schmidt, Ray. "Celebrating Michigan Flies and Tiers." 2009. http://www.facebook.com /note.php?note_id = 102634832924.

Schullery, Paul. "A Great Salesman." *American Angler*. 2007. http://www.american angler.com/history/a-great-salesman.

Sedgwick, Don, ed. *Joe Brooks on Fishing*. Guilford, CT: Lyons Press, 2004.

Smedley, Harold Hinsdill. *Fly Patterns and Their Origins*. 4th ed. Muskegon, MI: West-shore Publications, 1944.

———. *Trout of Michigan*. 2nd ed. Muskegon, MI: Westshore Publications, 1938.

Smith, Jeff. "Icons of the Fly Vest." *Traverse Magazine*. April 2009. Volume 28, number 11, pages 34–41.

About the Author and Illustrator

Jon Osborn has had articles published in *American Angler*, *Garden and Gun*, *The Upland Almanac*, and *The Tactical Edge* magazines and contributed to the book *American Blue*. Jon is a career police officer assigned to the patrol division and the tactical team. He divides his free time between his busy family and his passions for fly fishing and upland bird hunting. It's no secret that he wishes he could spend a decade or two angling alongside folks like Len Halladay and Clarence Roberts.

Jon welcomes your comments and questions at ozzy0908@hotmail.com.

Illustrator *Joe Van Faasen* is a product designer as well as an accomplished painter, working mostly in oils. His works can be found in private collections across the United States and in the Button-Petter Gallery. Worm dunking on inland lakes eventually led to fly-fishing the rivers in his home state, where a family cabin on the high banks of the Muskegon River fueled his love of the sport. Whether stalking nighttime browns during the Hex hatch or chasing salmon on "the Mo," Joe welcomes any chance he gets to cast a long rod. Joe also enjoys reading, tennis, and spending time with his young family.